Pebble® Plus
Bilingüe/Bilingual

Comida sana con MiPirámide/Healthy Eating with MyPyramid

El grupo de las carnes y los frijoles/
The Meat and Beans Group

por/by Mari C. Schuh

Traducción/Translation: Dr. Martín Luis Guzmán Ferrer
Editor Consultor/Consulting Editor: Dra. Gail Saunders-Smith

Consultor/Consultant: Barbara J. Rolls, PhD
Guthrie Chair in Nutrition
The Pennsylvania State University
University Park, Pennsylvania

Capstone press®
Mankato, Minnesota

Pebble Plus is published by Capstone Press,
151 Good Counsel Drive, P.O. Box 669, Mankato, Minnesota 56002.
www.capstonepress.com

1 2 3 4 5 6 11 10 09 08 07 06

Library of Congress Cataloging-in-Publication Data
Schuh, Mari C., 1975–
    [Meat and beans group. English & Spanish]
    El grupo de las carnes y los frijoles/de Mari C. Schuh = The meat and beans group/by Mari C. Schuh.
    p. cm.—(Comida sana con MiPirámide = Healthy eating with MyPyramid)
    title: Meat and beans group.
    Includes index.
    Parallel text in English and Spanish.
    ISBN-13: 978-0-7368-6668-2 (hardcover)
    ISBN-10: 0-7368-6668-X (hardcover)
    1. Meat—Juvenile literature. 2. Beans—Juvenile literature. 3. Nutrition—Juvenile literature. I. Title:
Meat and beans group. II. Title.
TX373.S3818 2007
641.3'6—dc22   2005037332

Summary: Simple text and photographs present the meat and beans group, the foods in this group, and
    examples of healthy eating choices—in both English and Spanish.

Credits
Katy Kudela, bilingual editor; Eida del Risco, Spanish copy editor; Jennifer Bergstrom, designer;
    Kelly Garvin, photo researcher; Stacy Foster and Michelle Biedscheid, photo shoot coordinators

Photo Credits
Capstone Press/Karon Dubke, all except U.S. Department of Agriculture, 8 (inset), 9 (computer screen)

Capstone Press thanks Hilltop Hy-Vee employees in Mankato, Minnesota, for their helpful assistance with
photo shoots.

**Information in this book supports the U.S. Department of Agriculture's MyPyramid for Kids
food guidance system found at http://www.MyPyramid.gov/kids. Food amounts listed in this
book are based on an 1,800-calorie food plan.**

**The U.S. Department of Agriculture (USDA) does not endorse any products, services,
or organizations.**

Note to Parents and Teachers

The Comida sana con MiPirámide/Healthy Eating with MyPyramid set supports national
science standards related to nutrition and physical health. This book describes and illustrates
the meat and beans group in both English and Spanish. The images support early readers in
understanding the text. The repetition of words and phrases helps early readers learn new
words. This book also introduces early readers to subject-specific vocabulary words, which
are defined in the Glossary section. Early readers may need assistance to read some words
and to use the Table of Contents, Glossary, Internet Sites, and Index sections of the book.

Table of Contents

Tabla de contenidos

The Meat and Beans Group

Have you eaten

any foods from the

meat and beans group today?

El grupo de las carnes y los frijoles

¿Has comido hoy alguno de

los alimentos del grupo de

las carnes y los frijoles?

Meat, chicken, fish.

Beans, eggs, nuts, and seeds.

These foods give you protein.

Carne, pollo, pescado.

Frijoles, huevos, nueces

y semillas. Todos estos

alimentos te dan proteínas.

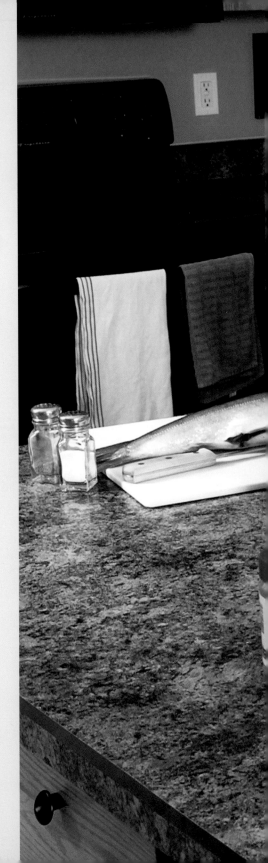

MyPyramid for Kids

MyPyramid is a tool to help you eat healthy food. The meat and beans group is part of MyPyramid.

MiPirámide para niños

MiPirámide es una herramienta que te ayuda a comer alimentos saludables. El grupo de las carnes y los frijoles es parte de MiPirámide.

MyPyramid For Kids
Eat Right. Exercise. Have Fun.

To learn more about
healthy eating,
go to this web site:
www.MyPyramid.gov/kids
Ask an adult for help.

Para saber más sobre
comida sana, ve a este
sitio de Internet:
www.MyPyramid.gov/kids
Pídele a un adulto
que te ayude.

9

Eat 5 ounces from

the meat and beans group

every day.

Come 5 onzas del grupo

de las carnes y los frijoles

todos los días.

Enjoying Meat and Beans

Some meats have lots of fat.

Low-fat meats are better for you.

Choose low-fat beef, chicken,

pork, turkey, and fish.

Cómo disfrutar de la carne y los frijoles

Algunas carnes tienen muchísima grasa.

Para ti las carnes bajas en grasa son las

mejores. Escoge las carnes bajas en grasa,

sean de res, pollo, cerdo, pavo o pescado.

Mankato's Finest Quality Meats!

LEAN GROUND BEEF 93/7

HONEYSUCKLE WHITE

13

Yum! Enjoy a sandwich
at lunch. If you want
to try a new food,
have a veggie burger.

¡Qué rico! En el almuerzo disfruta
de un sándwich. Si quieres probar
un nuevo alimento cómete una
hamburguesa de verduras.

Brrrrr! Warm up
with a bowl of chili
on a cold night.
Dig into the spicy meat
and beans.

¡Qué frío! Caliéntate con
un plato de chile con carne
en una noche fría. Saborea
la carne picante con frijoles.

Mixed nuts

make a crunchy snack.

Nuts have protein

and give you energy.

Las nueces constituyen

una merienda muy sabrosa.

Las nueces tienen proteínas

que te dan energía.

Foods from the
meat and beans group
are part of a healthy meal.
What are your favorites?

Los alimentos del grupo de
las carnes y los frijoles son
parte de una comida saludable.
¿Cuáles son tus favoritos?

How Much to Eat/Cuánto hay que comer

Many kids need to eat 5 ounces from the meat and beans group every day.
To get 5 ounces, pick five of your favorite foods below.

La mayoría de los niños necesitan 5 onzas diarias del grupo de las carnes y los frijoles.
Para completar 5 onzas, escoge cinco de tus favoritos entre los siguientes alimentos.

Pick five foods below to eat today!

¡Escoge cinco de estos alimentos para el día de hoy!

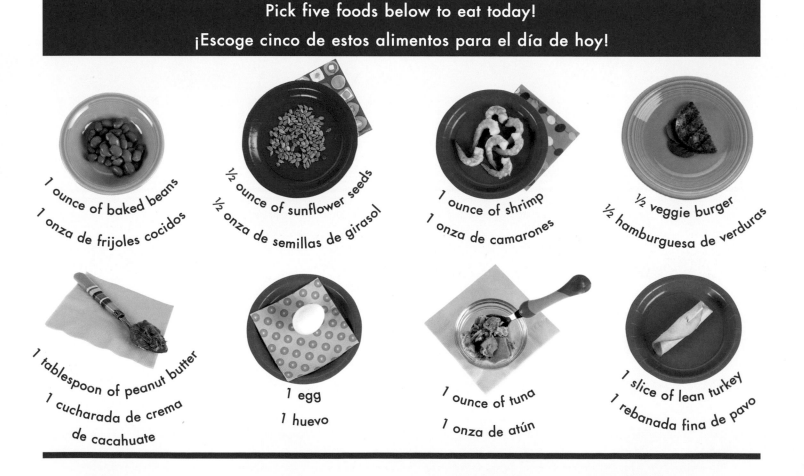

1 ounce of baked beans
1 onza de frijoles cocidos

½ ounce of sunflower seeds
½ onza de semillas de girasol

1 ounce of shrimp
1 onza de camarones

½ veggie burger
½ hamburguesa de verduras

1 tablespoon of peanut butter
1 cucharada de crema de cacahuate

1 egg
1 huevo

1 ounce of tuna
1 onza de atún

1 slice of lean turkey
1 rebanada fina de pavo

Glossary

energy—the strength to do active things without getting tired

MyPyramid—a food plan that helps kids make healthy food choices and reminds kids to be active; MyPyramid was created by the U.S. Department of Agriculture.

protein—a substance found in plant and animal cells; your body needs protein to work right.

Glosario

la energía—fuerza que te permite estar activo sin cansarte

MiPirámide—plan de alimentos que ayuda a los chicos a escoger comidas saludables y a mantenerse activos; MiPirámide fue creada por el Departamento de Agricultura de los Estados Unidos.

las proteínas—sustancia que se encuentra en las células de las plantas y los animales; tu cuerpo necesita proteínas para trabajar bien.

Index

Internet Sites

FactHound offers a safe, fun way to find Internet sites related to this book. All of the sites on FactHound have been researched by our staff.

Here's how:

1. Visit *www.facthound.com*

2. Choose your grade level.

3. Type in this book ID **073686668X** for age-appropriate sites. You may also browse subjects by clicking on letters, or by clicking on pictures and words.

4. Click on the **Fetch It** button.

FactHound will fetch the best sites for you!

Índice

Sitios de Internet

FactHound proporciona una manera divertida y segura de encontrar sitios de Internet relacionados con este libro. Nuestro personal ha investigado todos los sitios de FactHound. Es posible que los sitios no estén en español.

Se hace así:

1. Visita *www.facthound.com*

2. Elige tu grado escolar.

3. Introduce este código especial **073686668X** para ver sitios apropiados según tu edad, o usa una palabra relacionada con este libro para hacer una búsqueda general.

4. Haz clic en el botón **Fetch It**.

¡FactHound buscará los mejores sitios para ti!